THE EURHYTHMICS
OF JAQUES-DALCROZE

MORE WILDSIDE CLASSICS

Please see www.wildsidepress.com for a complete list!

THE EURHYTHMICS OF JAQUES-DALCROZE

EMILE JAQUES-DALCROZE

WILDSIDE PRESS

THE EURHYTHMICS OF JAQUES-DALCROZE

This edition published in 2007 by Wildside Press, LLC.
www.wildsidebooks.com

FOREWORD

"Rhythmische Gymnastik" is the name by which the Dalcroze method is known in Germany, but whether or not the German words are adequate, their literal translation into English certainly gives too narrow an idea of the scope of the system to any one unacquainted with it. Rhythmical "gymnastics," in the natural meaning of the word, is a part of the Dalcroze training, and a not unimportant part, but it is only one application of a much wider principle; and accordingly, where the term occurs in the following pages, it must be understood simply as denoting a particular mode of physical drill. But for the principle itself and the total method embodying it, another name is needed, and the term "Eurhythmics" has been here coined for the purpose. The originality of the Dalcroze method, the fact that it is a discovery, gives it a right to a name of its own: it is because it is in a sense also the rediscovery of an old secret that a name has been chosen of such plain reference and derivation. Plato, in the words quoted above, has said that the whole of a man's life stands in need of a right rhythm: and it is natural to see some kinship between this Platonic attitude and the claim of Dalcroze that his discovery is not a mere refinement of dancing, nor an improved method of music-teaching, but a principle that must have effect upon every part of life.

John W. Harvey.

CONTENTS

THE EDUCATIONAL SIGNIFICANCE OF HELLERAU

At Hellerau two things make an ineffaceable impression upon the mind—the exquisite beauty of movement, of gesture and of grouping seen in the exercises; and the nearness of a great force, fundamental to the arts and expressing itself in the rhythm to which they attain. Jaques-Dalcroze has re-opened a door which has long been closed. He has rediscovered one of the secrets of Greek education.

A hundred years ago Wilhelm von Humboldt endeavoured to make Greek ideals the paramount influence in the higher schools of Germany. He and a group of friends had long felt indignant at the utilitarianism and shallowness of the work of the schools. In Greek literature, Greek philosophy and Greek art would be found a means of kindling new life in education and of giving it the power of building up strong and independent personalities. When there came to Humboldt the unexpected opportunity of reforming the secondary schools of Prussia, he so remodelled the course of study as to secure for Greek thought and letters a place which, if not central and determinative, would at least bring the élite of the younger generation in some measure under their influence. But his administrative orders failed to impart to the schools the spirit of ancient Greece. To Humboldt and his friends Greek studies had been an inspiration because, apart from their intellectual significance and literary form, those studies had been the channel of an artistic impulse and had been entered into as art. But this artistic power was not felt by the greater number of those who undertook, in obedience to the new regulations, the duty of teaching Greek in the schools. What was left in Greek studies after this failure of artistic insight was often no more than another form of purely intellectual discipline. A new subject had been added to the curriculum, but new life had not been brought into the schools. The very name, Gymnasium, which denoted their Hellenic purpose, seemed ironical. They were not Greek in spirit and they ignored the training of the body. Thus what Wilhelm von Humboldt had chiefly aimed at accomplishing, he failed to do. It was not the power of Greek art that he brought into the schools but, in most cases, merely the philological study of a second dead language. The cause of his failure was that he had not discovered the educational method which could effectually secure his purpose. He had assumed that, in order to introduce the Greek spirit into education, it was sufficient to insist upon the linguistic and literary study of Greek.

In time, attempts were made to remedy what was defective in Humboldt's plan by insisting upon physical exercises as an obligatory part of education in the higher schools. But the physical exercises thus introduced, though salutary in themselves, were divorced from the artistic influences of the Greek gymnastic. Humboldt's chief aim had been forgotten. His system of organization had rooted itself, but his educational ideal, to which he attached far greater importance than to administrative regulation, was ignored.

In later years, though such Neo-Hellenism as Humboldt's had long gone out of fashion, the weakness of the higher schools on the side of artistic training was recognized. But a corrective for this was sought in instruction about art, not (except so far as a little teaching of drawing went) in the practice of an art. An attempt was made to cultivate aesthetic appreciation by lessons which imparted knowledge but did not attempt to train the power of artistic production—an aim which was regarded as unrealizable, except in vocal music, and of course through literary composition, in a secondary school. Thus Humboldt's original purpose has been almost wholly unachieved. The schools, admirably organized on the intellectual side and, within certain limits, increasingly efficient in their physical training, are, as a rule, lacking in the influence of art, as indeed in most cases are the corresponding schools in other countries. The spring of artistic training has not been touched. The divorce between intellectual discipline and artistic influence (except indeed so far as the latter is operative through the study of literature, through a little drawing, and through vocal music) is complete. This defect is felt even more keenly in Germany than in England, because in the German schools the intellectual pressure is more severe, and the schools do less for the cultivation of those interests which lie outside the limits of regular class-room work.

Wilhelm von Humboldt gave little direct attention to the work of the elementary schools. His chief concern was with higher education. But in the elementary schools also, except in so far as they gave much care to vocal music, the course of training failed to make use of the educative power of art. A conviction that there is an error has led in Germany, as in England and America, to an increased attention to drawing and to attempts to interest children in good pictures. But there is still (except in the case of vocal music and a little drawing) an unbridged gap between the intellectual and the artistic work of the schools.

Jaques-Dalcroze's experience suggests the possibility of a much closer combination of these two elements, both in elementary and in secondary education. His teaching requires from the pupils a sustained and careful attention, is in short a severe (though not exhausting) intellectual exercise; while at the same time it trains the sense of form and rhythm, the capacity to analyse musical structure, and the power of expressing rhythm through harmonious movement. It is thus a synthesis of educational influence, artistic and intellectual. Its educational value for young children, its applicability to their needs, the pleasure which they take in the exercises, have been conclusively proved. And in the possibility of this widely extended use of the method lies perhaps the chief, though far indeed from the only, educational significance of what is now being done at Hellerau.

M. E. Sadler.

RHYTHM AS A FACTOR IN EDUCATION
FROM THE FRENCH OF
E. JAQUES-DALCROZE[1]

It is barely a hundred years since music ceased to be an aristocratic art cultivated by a few privileged individuals and became instead a subject of instruction for almost everybody without regard to talent or exceptional ability. Schools of Music, formerly frequented only by born musicians, gifted from birth with unusual powers of perception for sound and rhythm, to-day receive all who are fond of music, however little Nature may have endowed them with the necessary capacity for musical expression and realization. The number of solo players, both pianists and violinists, is constantly increasing, instrumental technique is being developed to an extraordinary degree, but everywhere, too, the question is being asked whether the quality of instrumental players is equal to their quantity, and whether the acquirement of extraordinary technique is likely to help musical progress when this technique is not joined to musical powers, if not of the first rank, at least normal.

Of ten certificated pianists of to-day, at the most one, if indeed one, is capable of recognizing one key from another, of improvising four bars with character or so as to give pleasure to the listener, of giving expression to a composition without the help of the more or less numerous annotations with which present day composers have to burden their work, of experiencing any feeling whatever when they listen to, or perform, the composition of another. The solo players of older days were without exception complete musicians, able to improvise and compose, artists driven irresistibly towards art by a noble thirst for aesthetic expression, whereas most young people who devote themselves nowadays to solo playing have the gifts neither of hearing nor of expression, are content to imitate the composer's expression without the power of feeling it, and have no other sensibility than that of the fingers, no other motor faculty than an automatism painfully acquired. Solo playing of the present day has specialized in a finger technique which takes no account of the faculty of

1   First published in *Le Rhythme* (Bâle) of December, 1909.

mental expression. It is no longer a means, it has become an end.

As a rule, writing is only taught to children who have reached a thinking age, and we do not think of initiating them into the art of elocution until they have got something to say, until their powers of comprehension, analysis and feeling begin to show themselves. All modern educationalists are agreed that the first step in a child's education should be to teach him to know himself, to accustom him to life and to awaken in him sensations, feelings and emotions, before giving him the power of describing them. Likewise, in modern methods of teaching to draw, the pupil is taught to see objects before painting them. In music, unfortunately, the same rule does not hold. Young people are taught to play the compositions of Bach, Mozart, Beethoven, Chopin and Liszt, before their minds and ears can grasp these works, before they have developed the faculty of being moved by them.

There are two physical agents by means of which we appreciate music. These two agents are the ear as regards sound, and the whole nervous system as regards rhythm. Experience has shown me that the training of these two agents cannot easily be carried out simultaneously. A child finds it difficult to appreciate at the same time a succession of notes forming a melody and the rhythm which animates them.

Before teaching the relation which exists between sound and movement, it is wise to undertake the independent study of each of these two elements. Tone is evidently secondary, since it has not its origin and model in ourselves, whereas movement is instinctive in man and therefore primary. Therefore I begin the study of music by careful and experimental teaching of movement. This is based in earliest childhood on the automatic exercise of marching, for marching is the natural model of time measure.

By means of various accentuations with the foot, I teach the different time measures. Pauses (of varying lengths) in the marching teach the children to distinguish durations of sound; movements to time with the arms and the head preserve order in the succession of the time measures and analyse the bars and pauses.

All this, no doubt, seems very simple, and so I thought when beginning my experiments. Unfortunately, the latter have shown me that it is not so simple as it seems, but on the contrary very complicated. And this because most children have no instinct for time, for time values, for accentuation, for physical balance; because the motor faculties are not the same in all individuals, and because a number of obstacles impede the exact and rapid physical realization of mental conceptions. One child is always behind the beat when marching, another always ahead; another takes unequal steps, another on the contrary lacks balance. All these faults, if not corrected in the first years, will reappear later in the musical technique of the individual.

Unsteady time when singing or playing, confusion in playing, inability to follow when accompanying, accentuating too roughly or with lack of precision, all these faults have their origin in the child's muscular and nervous control, in lack of co-ordination between the mind which conceives, the brain which orders, the nerve which transmits and the muscle which executes. And still more, the power of phrasing and shading music with feeling depends equally upon the training of the nerve-centres, upon the co-ordination of the muscular system, upon rapid communication between brain and limbs—in a word, upon the health of the whole organism; and it is by trying to discover the individual cause of each musical defect, and to find a means of correcting it, that I have gradually built up my method of eurhythmics.

This method is entirely based upon experiments many times repeated, and not one of the exercises has been adopted until it has been applied under different forms and under different conditions and its usefulness definitely proved. Many people have a completely false idea of my system, and consider it is a simple variant on the methods of physical training at present in fashion, whose inventors have undoubtedly rendered great service to humanity.

I cannot help smiling when I read in certain papers, over names which carry weight, articles in which my method is compared to other gymnastic systems. The fact is, my book is simply a register of the different exercises which I have invented, and says nothing of my ideas in general, for it is written for those who have learnt to interpret my meaning under my personal tuition at Geneva and Hellerau.

Quite naturally, half the critics who have done me the honour of discussing the book, have only glanced through it and looked at the photographs. Not one of them has undergone the special training upon which I lay stress and without which I deny absolutely that any one has the right to pass a definite judgment on my meaning; for one does not learn to ride by reading a book on horsemanship, and eurhythmics are above all a matter of personal experience.

The object of the method is, in the first instance, to create by the help of rhythm a rapid and regular current of communication between brain and body; and what differentiates my physical exercises from those of present-day methods of muscular development is that each of them is conceived in the form which can most quickly establish in the brain the image of the movement studied.

It is a question of eliminating in every muscular movement, by the help of will, the untimely intervention of muscles useless for the movement in question, and thus developing attention, consciousness and will-power. Next must be created an automatic technique for all those muscular movements which do not need the help of the consciousness, so that the latter may be reserved for those forms of expression which are purely intelligent. Thanks to the co-ordination of the nerve-centres, to the formation and development of the greatest possible number of motor habits, my method assures the freest possible play to subconscious expression. The creation in the organism of a rapid and easy means of communication between thought and its means of expression by movements allows the personality free play, giving it character, strength and life to an extraordinary degree.

Neurasthenia is often nothing else than intellectual confusion produced by the inability of the nervous system to obtain from the muscular system regular obedience to the order from the brain. Training the nerve centres, establishing order in the organism, is the only remedy for intellectual perversion produced by lack of will power and by the incomplete subjection of body to mind. Unable to obtain physical realization of its ideas, the brain amuses itself in forming images without hope of realizing them, drops the real for the unreal, and substitutes vain and vague speculation for the free and healthy union of mind and body.

The first result of a thorough rhythmic training is that the pupil sees clearly in himself what he really is, and obtains from his powers all the advantage possible. This result seems to me one which should attract the attention of all educationalists and assure to education by and for rhythm an important place in general culture.

But, as an artist, I wish to add, that the second result of this education ought to be to put the completely developed faculties of the individual at the service of art and to give the latter the most subtle and complete of interpreters—the human body. For the body can become a marvellous instrument of beauty and harmony when it vibrates in tune with artistic imagination and collaborates with creative thought. It is not enough that, thanks to special exercises, students of music should have corrected their faults and be no longer in danger of spoiling their musical interpretations by their lack of physical skill and harmonious movements; it is necessary in addition that the music which lives within them—artists will understand me—should obtain free and complete development, and that the rhythms which inspire their personality should enter into intimate communion with those which animate the works to be interpreted.

The education of the nervous system must be of such a nature that the suggested rhythms of a work of art induce in the individual analogous vibrations, produce a powerful reaction in him and change naturally into rhythms of expression. In simpler language, the body must become capable of responding to artistic rhythms and of realizing them quite naturally without fear of exaggeration.

This faculty of emotion, indispensable to the artist, was formerly natural to almost all beginners in music, for hardly any but pre-destined artists devoted themselves to the art; but, if this is no longer the case, it is possible at least to awaken dulled faculties, to develop and co-ordinate them, and it is the duty of every musical educationalist to deter from instrumental technique every individual who is still without musical feeling.

The experimental study of rhythm should form a part of every well-organized musical education, and this study will be useful not only to musicians, but to music itself. It is quite certain that, if since Beethoven's time harmony has developed, if each generation has created fresh groupings of sounds, it is not the same regarding rhythmic forms, which remain much as they were.

I shall be told that the means of expression are of no importance so long as the artist is able to show his meaning, that a sincere emotion can be clearly expressed even with old-fashioned rhythms, and that to try and create new rhythms is mere technical work, and to enforce such upon the composers of to-morrow is simply depriving them of their character. This is all true, and I myself have a horror of seeking new means of expression within the limits of hard and fast rules, for expression ought to be a spontaneous manifestation. But I assert that experiments in rhythm, and the complete study of movements simple and combined, ought to create a fresh mentality, that artists thus trained will find inevitably and spontaneously new rhythmic forms to express their feelings, and that in consequence their characters will be able to develop more completely and with greater strength. It is a fact that very young children taught by my method invent quite naturally physical rhythms such as would have occurred to very few professional musicians, and that my most advanced pupils find monotonous many contemporary works the rhythmic poverty of which shocks neither public nor critics.

I will terminate this short sketch of my system by pointing out the intimate relations which exist between movements in time and movements in space, between rhythms in sound and rhythm in the body, between Music and Plastic Expression.

Gestures and attitudes of the body complete, animate and enliven any rhythmic music written simply and naturally without special regard to tone, and, just as in painting there exist side by side a school of the nude and a school of landscape, so in music there may be developed, side by side, plastic music and music pure and simple. In the school of landscape painting emotion is created entirely by combinations of moving light and by the rhythms thus caused. In the school of the nude, which pictures the many shades of expression of the human body, the artist tries to show the human soul as expressed by physical forms, enlivened by the emotions of the moment, and at the same time the characteristics suitable to the individual and his race, such as they appear through momentary physical modifications.

In the same way, plastic music will picture human feelings expressed by gesture and will model its sound forms on those of rhythms derived directly from expressive movements of the human body.

To compose the music which the Greeks appear to have realized, and for which Goethe and Schiller hoped, musicians must have acquired experience of physical movements; this, however, is certainly not the case to-day, for music has become beyond all others an intellectual art. While awaiting this transformation, present generations can apply education by and for rhythm to the interpretation of plastic stage music such as Richard Wagner has imagined. At the present day this music is not interpreted at all, for dramatic singers, stage managers and conductors do not understand the relation existing between gesture and music, and the absolute ignorance regarding plastic expression which characterizes the lyric actors of our day is a real profanation of scenic musical art. Not only are singers allowed to walk and gesticulate on the stage without paying any attention to the time, but also no shade of expression, dynamic or motor, of the orchestra—crescendo, decrescendo, accelerando, rallentando—finds in their gestures adequate realization. By this I mean the kind of wholly instinctive transformation of sound movements into bodily movements such as my method teaches.

Authors, poets, musicians and painters cannot demand from

the interpreters of their works knowledge of the relations between movements in time and in space, for this knowledge can only be developed by special studies. No doubt a few poets and painters have an inborn knowledge of the rhythms of space; for instance, Hugo von Hofmannsthal, the stage mounter of "Electra" at the Vienna Opera, who constructed a huge staircase, on which, however, the actors, having little acquaintance with the most elementary notions of balance, moved with deplorable heaviness; or again, the aesthetician Adolphe Appia, whose remarkable work *Music and Stage Mounting* ought to be the guide of all stage managers. But the majority of composers write their plastic music without knowing whether it is capable of being practically realized, without personal experience of the laws of weight, force and bodily movement.

My hope is, that sincere artists desirous of perfection and seeking progress will study seriously the grave question which I raise. For my own part, relying on many experiments, and full of confidence in ideas carefully thought out, I have devoted my life to the teaching of rhythm, being fully satisfied that, thanks to it, man will regain his natural powers of expression, and at the same time his full motor faculties, and that art has everything to hope from new generations brought up in the cult of harmony, of physical and mental health, of order, beauty and truth.

FROM THE LECTURES OF EMILE JAQUES-DALCROZE

(Lecture at Leipzig, December 10, 1911)

The objection is often raised that under my system the technique of an instrument is acquired too late. But this objection has no foundation in fact. A child who begins rhythmic gymnastics as I would have it in its fifth or sixth year and a year later ear-training, can certainly have piano lessons when eight years old, and I can state from experience that the finger technique of the child will then develop much more quickly, for the musical faculties in general will have been far better developed, more thoroughly trained and become more part of the child's life owing to the preliminary training.

*****

Lessons in rhythmic gymnastics help children in their other lessons, for they develop the powers of observation, of analyzing, of understanding and of memory, thus making them more orderly and precise.

*****

The effect of rhythmic training on the time-table and life of a school is like that of a hot water heating system which spreads an equal warmth through all parts of a building. Teachers of other subjects will find that such training provides them with pupils more responsive, more elastic and of more character than they otherwise would be. Therefore, the study of rhythm, as well as education by means of rhythm, ought to be most closely connected with school life.

(Address to the Dresden Teachers' Association, May 28, 1912)

From many years' experience of music teaching I have gradually produced a method which gives a child musical experiences instead of musical knowledge.

I expect much from education in rhythm in elementary schools, provided it be given regularly, completely and sufficiently. The exercises should be begun at the age of six, with half an hour's lesson three times a week, but these lessons can quite well be taken from playtime. By the age of twelve two lessons a week are sufficient. This training will not only develop the feeling for beauty and form by accustoming the eye to distinguish beautiful movements and lines from those that are ugly, but also render the children susceptible to musical impressions.

There are always children who are not able to sing in time, or even to beat time, to walk in time, or to graduate the strength and rapidity of their movements. Such children are unrhythmic, and it will generally be noticed that these children are stiff and awkward,

THE SCHOOL

often also over-excitable. This lack of rhythm is almost like a disease. It is caused by the lack of balance between the mental and physical powers, which results from insufficient co-ordination between the mental picture of a movement and its performance by the body, and these nervous troubles are just as much the cause as the result of such lack of harmony. In some cases the brain gives clear and definite impulses, but the limbs, in themselves healthy, can do nothing because the nervous system is in confusion. In other cases the limbs have lost the power to carry out orders sent by the brain, and the undischarged nerve-impulses disturb the whole nervous system. In other cases again, muscles and nerves are healthy, but insufficient training in rhythm impedes the formation of lasting rhythmic images in the brain. To repeat, the causes of this lack of rhythm all lie in the important but insufficiently recognized psycho-physiological sphere of the co-ordination of brain, nerve-paths and muscles.

The objection is sometimes made that rhythmic gymnastics cause nerve-strain in children. This is not the case. Several brain specialists have told me that they have effected satisfactory cures with rhythmic gymnastic exercises.

Rhythm is infinite, therefore the possibilities for physical representations of rhythm are infinite.

(Address to Students, *der Rhythmus*, Vol. I, p. 41, *et seq.*)

I consider it unpardonable that in teaching the piano the whole attention should be given to the imitative faculties, and that the pupil should have no opportunity whatever of expressing his own musical impressions with the technical means which are taught him.

Whether the teacher himself be a genius is of little importance, provided he is able to help others to develop their own talents.

One can create nothing of lasting value without self-knowledge. The only living art is that which grows out of one's own experiences. It is just the same with teaching; it is quite impossible to develop others until one has proved one's own powers in every direction, until one has learnt to conquer oneself, to make oneself better, to suppress bad tendencies, to strengthen good ones, and, in the place of the primitive being, to make one more complete who, having consciously formed himself, knows his powers. Only in proportion as one develops oneself is one able to help others to develop.

I consider that one does not require to be a genius in order to teach others, but that one certainly does require strong conviction, enthusiasm, persistence and joy in life. All these qualities are equally derived from the control and knowledge of self.

We must, from youth upwards, learn that we are masters of our fate, that heredity is powerless if we realize that we can conquer it, that our future depends upon the victory which we gain over ourselves. However weak the individual may be, his help is required to prepare a way for a better future. Life and growth are one and the same, and it is our duty by the example of our lives to develop those who come after us. Let us therefore assume the responsibility which Nature puts upon us, and consider it our duty to regenerate ourselves; thus shall we help the growth of a more beautiful humanity.

I like joy, for it is life. I preach joy, for it alone gives the power of creating useful and lasting work. Amusement, an excitement which stimulates the nerves instead of uplifting the spirit, is not necessary in the life of the artist. Of course one must often let oneself go, and I should be the last to defend a so-called moral discipline, or a pedantic rule of monastic severity. For a healthy, active person the joy of the daily struggle and of work performed with enthusiasm should be sufficient to beautify life, drive away fatigue and illuminate present and future. This condition of joy is

THE COLLEGE

brought about in us by the feeling of freedom and responsibility, by the clear perception of the creative power in us, by the balance of our natural powers, by the harmonious rhythm between intention and deed. It depends upon our creative faculties, both natural and acquired, and becomes greater as these grow. The power of understanding ourselves certainly gives us a sense of freedom, for it opens a rapid correspondence, not only between imagination and power of performance, between apperception and feelings, but also between the various kinds of feelings which dwell in us.

THE JAQUES-DALCROZE
METHOD

I. GROWTH[2]

Emile Jaques-Dalcroze was born in Vienna on July 6, 1865, of mixed parentage, his father being a Swiss from St. Croix in the Jura (hence the artist name Dalcroze), his mother of German extraction. At the age of eight his parents brought him to Geneva, where in due course he became a student at the Conservatoire of Music. His musical education was continued in Paris under Léo Delibes and in Vienna under Bruckner and Fuchs. For a short period his studies were interrupted by an engagement as musical director of a small theatre in Algiers—an opportunity which he used for study of the peculiar rhythms of Arab popular music, which he found unusually interesting and stimulating.

Returning to Geneva, he earned, by a life of varied activities as teacher, writer and composer, a standing which in 1892 brought him the appointment of Professor of Harmony at the Geneva Conservatoire.

The wider experience which the new sphere of work brought was to a certain extent a disappointment, for with it came clear evidence of what had before only been suspected, namely, that the education of future professional musicians was in many ways radically wrong, in that the training of individual faculties was made the chief object, without consideration of whether or no these faculties stood in any close relation to the inner consciousness of the student. In other words, the aim of the training was to form means of expression, without consideration of what was to be expressed, to produce a highly trained instrument, without thought of the art whose servant it was to be, to take as primary object a thing of secondary importance, indeed only of importance at all when consequent on something which the usual training entirely neglected. The students were taught to play instruments, to sing songs, but

---

2   For much of the material of this chapter the writer is indebted to Herr Karl Storck, of Berlin, to whose book *E. Jaques-Dalcroze, seine Stellung und Aufgabe in unserer Zeit*, Stuttgart, 1912, Greiner & Pfeiffer, the reader is directed.

without any thought of such work becoming a means of self expression and so it was found that pupils, technically far advanced, after many years of study were unable to deal with the simplest problems in rhythm and that their sense for pitch, relative or absolute, was most defective; that, while able to read accurately or to play pieces memorized, they, had not the slightest power of giving musical expression to their simplest thoughts or feelings, in fact were like people who possess the vocabulary of a language and are able to read what others have written, yet are unable to put their own simple thoughts and impressions into words. The analogy here is the simplest use of everyday language; from this to the art of the essayist or poet is far; so in music—one who has mastered notes, chords and rhythms can give musical expression to simple thoughts and feelings, while to become a composer he must traverse a road that only natural talent can render easy.

Jaques-Dalcroze took the view that technique should be nothing but a means to art, that the aim of musical education should be, not the production of pianists, violinists, singers, but of musically developed human beings, and that therefore the student should not begin by specializing on any instrument, but by developing his musical faculties, thus producing a basis for specialized study. This training could only be obtained by awakening the sense, natural though often latent, for the ultimate bases of music, namely, *tone* and *rhythm*. As the sense for tone could only be developed through the ear, he now gave special attention to vocal work, and noticed that when the students themselves beat time to their singing, the work became much more real, that the pupils had a feeling of being physically in unison with the music, indeed the feeling of producing something complete and beautiful. Following up this hint, "Gesture Songs" were written, which, it was found, were performed with surprising ease.

Up to this point movement had only been used as an accompaniment to music, not as a means of expressing it; the next step was to give the body a training so refined and so detailed as to make it sensitive to every rhythmic impulse and able to lose itself in any music. This co-ordination of movement and music is the essence of the Jaques-Dalcroze method, and differentiates it from all other methods of similar aim.

So far only arm movements had been employed, and those merely the conventional ones of the conductor. The next step was to devise a series of arm movements, providing a means of clearly marking all tempi from two beats in the bar to twelve beats in the bar, including such forms as 5/4 7/4 9/4 11/4, and a system of movements of the body and lower limbs to represent time values from any number of notes to the beat up to whole notes of twelve beats to the note. From the first the work aroused keen interest among the students and their parents, and the master was given enthusiastic help by them in all his experiments; above all he was loyally aided by his assistant, Fräulein Nina Gorter. The Conservatoire authorities, however, were not sympathetic, and it became necessary to form a volunteer-experimental class, which worked outside official hours and buildings.

The first public recognition of the method was at the Music Festival in Solothurn in 1905, where a demonstration was given which made a striking impression on those present. The value of the method for the elementary education of musicians was immediately recognized and some slight idea obtained of the part it might play in general elementary education. It has been made clear that the method had its origin in the attempt to give life and reality to musical education, to give a foundational development on which specialized music study could be based, and that it had grown naturally and gradually as the result of observation and experiment. Now it began to be apparent that something still greater than the original aim had been achieved, that the system evolved was one which, properly used, might be of enormous value in the education of children. With characteristic energy Jaques-Dalcroze, inspired by the new idea, took up the study of psychology, in which he was helped by his friend, the psychologist Claparède, who early saw the value which the new ideas might have in educational practice. The change of outlook which now took place in the master's mind can best be made clear by a translation of his own words.[3]

> "It is true that I first devised my method as a musician for musicians. But the further I carried my experiments, the more I noticed that, while a method intended to develop the sense for rhythm, and indeed based on such development, is of great importance in the education of a musician, its chief value lies in the fact that it trains the powers of apperception and of expression in the individual and renders easier the externalization of natural emo-

---

3   Address to students, Dresden, 1911 (*Der Rhythmus*, vol. i, p. 33).

tions. Experience teaches me that a man is not ready for the specialized study of an art until his character is formed, and his powers of expression developed."

In 1906 was held the first training-course for teachers; how the method has since grown can be realized by noting that a fortnight was then considered a sufficient period of training, whilst now the teachers' course at Hellerau requires from one to three years' steady work. In the years 1907-9 the short teachers' courses were repeated; in the latter year the first diploma was granted, experience having shown the need of this, for already individuals in all parts of the world, after but a few days' training, in some cases after merely being spectators at lessons, were advertising themselves as teachers of the method. In 1910 Jaques-Dalcroze was invited by the brothers Wolf and Harald Dohrn to come to Dresden, where, in the garden suburb of Hellerau, they have built him a College for Rhythmic Training, a true Palace of Rhythm.

II. PRACTICE[4]

The method naturally falls into three divisions—

- (*a*) Rhythmic gymnastics proper.
- (*b*) Ear training.
- (*c*) Improvisation (practical harmony).

(*a*) Is essentially the Jaques-Dalcroze method—that which is fundamentally new. As it is this part of the method which is likely to prove of great value in all systems of education, not merely as a preparation for the study of music, but as a means to the utmost development of faculty in the individual, it will be dealt with in detail.

(*b*) Is of the greatest importance as an adjunct to rhythmic gymnastics, since it is through the ear that rhythm-impressions are most often and most easily obtained. Jaques-Dalcroze naturally uses his own methods of ear-training, which are extremely

---

4   In the preparation of this chapter free use has been made of the writings of M. Jaques-Dalcroze and of Dr. Wolf Dohrn, Director of the College of Music and Rhythm, Hellerau, Dresden.

successful, but he does not lay stress on them; he does, however, emphasize the need of such training, whatever the method, as shall give the pupil an accurate sense of pitch, both absolute and relative, and a feeling for tonality. The more these are possessed the greater the use which can be made of rhythmic gymnastics.

(c) This is not required in the *pupil*, however valuable it may be as an additional means of self-expression; it is, however, abso-

Beating 4/4.

lutely necessary for the successful *teacher* of rhythmic gymnastics, who must be able to express, on some instrument—most conveniently the piano—whatever rhythms, simple or compound, he may wish to use in the training of his pupils. This subject, therefore, naturally forms an important part of the normal course at the Hellerau College, since this course is planned to meet the needs of students preparing for the teaching diploma in Eurhythmics. Here, too, Jaques-Dalcroze has his own system, with which he obtains results often remarkable, but, as in the case of the ear-training, this is a detail not peculiar to the method as a whole.

To repeat: the essentials are that the teacher have the power of free expression on some musical instrument, the pupil that of hearing correctly.

Movements for the Semibreve.

*****

The system of exercises known as rhythmic gymnastics is based upon two ideas, (i) *time* is shown by movements of the arms, (ii) *time-values*, i.e., note-duration, by movements of the feet and body. In the early stages of the training this principle is clearly observed; later it may be varied in many ingenious ways, for instance in what is known as plastic counterpoint, where the actual notes played are represented by movements of the arms, while the counterpoint in crotchets, quavers or semiquavers, is given by the feet.

The system of beating time with the arms provides for all tempi from 2/4 to 12/4 and includes 5/4 7/4 9/4.

In the series of movements to represent note-values the crotchet is taken as the unit; this is represented by a step; higher values, from the minim to the whole note of twelve beats, are represented by a step with one foot and a movement or movements with the other foot or with the body, but without progression, e.g., a minim by one step and a knee bend, a dotted minim by a step and two movements without progression, a whole note of twelve beats by a step and eleven movements. Thus for each note in the music there is one step, one progression in space, while at the same time the note, if of greater length than a crotchet, is analysed into crotchets.

Notes of shorter duration than the crotchet, i.e., quavers, triplets, etc., are expressed also by steps which become quicker in proportion to their frequency.

When the movements corresponding to the notes from the crotchet to the whole note of twelve beats have, with all their details, become a habit, the pupil need only make them mentally, contenting himself with one step forward. This step will have the exact length of the whole note, which will be mentally analysed into its various elements. Although these elements are not individually performed by the body, their images and the innervations suggested by those images take the place of the movements.

The process is similar to that of the child learning to read; at first it reads aloud, then to itself, still, however, moving its lips, i.e., still making all the innervations necessary for the pronunciation of the words. Only after much practice does the process become sufficiently automatic for these lip and tongue innervations to be dropped. Indeed, many adults show traces of them when they read. To what degree our power to read is based upon such innervations is shown by the fact that old people, as their inhibitory powers become weaker, often revert to making these lip movements. From this we may conclude that such innervations, although they do not find their natural expression, still exist and have effect, i.e., they are necessary. The Jaques Dalcroze method aims at nothing more or less than the training of rhythmic innervations.

The whole training aims at developing the power of rapid physical reaction to mental impressions. These latter are more commonly obtained through the ear, chiefly from the music played; naturally, however, the teacher needs at times to give commands during an exercise. For this purpose he invariably uses the word *hopp*, a word chosen for its clear incisiveness.

Before each exercise it is clearly stated what the word is to represent in that particular case, e.g., omit one beat, omit one bar, beat time twice as fast with the arms, etc.; often the word will be used in series in an exercise, each *hopp* meaning some additional change. As the command generally falls on the second half of the beat preceding the one in which the change is to be made, very rapid mental and physical response is necessary, especially if the music be at all quick. Exercises of this class soon give the power of rapid muscular innervation and inhibition, and are of extraordinary value in education, quite apart from their purely rhythmic side.

We will now consider the exercises in some detail, taking, as a matter of convenience, the order and grouping generally adopted at demonstrations of the method. In actual practice such strict grouping is neither possible nor necessary; the actual form which the lessons take will depend upon the genius of teacher and pupils, the possibilities of variety being infinite.

MOVEMENTS TO INDICATE VARIOUS TEMPI

Simple music is played to which the pupils march. As they grasp the beat they mark it by an accented step; when this becomes easy, the corresponding arm movements are added, and the strong beat, at this stage always the first, is marked by full contraction of the arm muscles. Practice is given until at *hopp* the pupil can stop suddenly, discontinue accenting with one or both arms or with one or both feet, substitute an arm-movement for a foot movement, insert an extra accent either with arm or foot, or do any similar thing previously agreed on. By repeated practice of such exercises complete automatic control of the limbs is obtained and the ground prepared for more advanced work. It is at this stage that the simple movements to indicate times and notes are learnt; they may be likened to the alphabet of the method, the elementary exercises as a whole being its accidence, the more advanced stages, including plastic expression, its syntax.

TRAINING IN METRE

This group of exercises is a natural extension of those preceding.

The pupil learns a series of movements which together form a rhythm, first practising them singly, then in groups, the signal for the change being always the word *hopp*. By means of such exercises the component movements required in the physical expression of a rhythm can be learnt, first individually, then in series, until the complete rhythm can be expressed and the use of *hopp* be dropped, each change of movement becoming itself the signal for the next.

Again, the pupil learns to realize[5] a rhythm played on the piano or indicated by the movements of another person. This is something quite apart from mere imitation; trained by previous exercises, the pupil first forms clear mental images of the movements corresponding to the rhythm in question and then gives physical expression to those images. In other words, he does not reproduce until he has understood; in fact, without understanding, correct reproduction of a lengthy series of such movements is impossible. In the same way, an individual cannot easily remember and repeat a succession of words which he does not understand, but can repeat without difficulty a long series of words of which he understands the sense. Indeed, the importance of many of these exercises becomes clearer when the way in which children are taught to read and write is remembered.

Oral and visual images of letters and words are impressed on the child by reading aloud, and in this way the young brain easily masters the difficult work of reading and writing. The Jaques-Dalcroze method proceeds in exactly the same manner as regards the elements of music.

When we have once realized this point, we are bound to wonder why music teaching has not always been based on this elementary and unfailing form. What would be said to teachers who tried to teach children to read and write without letting them spell and read aloud? But this is what has often been done in the teaching of music, and if children generally show but little pleasure and interest in their first music lessons, the fault does not lie with them but with our wrong method of making the elements clear to them.

As a matter of fact we generally do not make the latter clear to them, and fail in the most important duty of the educator and teacher, namely, that of making the child really experience what he is to learn.

DEVELOPMENT OF MENTAL RESPONSE

A rhythm in music consists of a regularly recurring series of accented sounds, unaccented sounds, and rests, expressed in

---

5   *Realize* is used in rhythmic gymnastics in the sense *express by movements of the body.*

rhythmic gymnastics by movements and inhibitions of movements. Individuals who are rhythmically uncertain generally have a muscular system which is irregularly responsive to mental stimuli; the response may be too rapid or too slow; in either case impulse or inhibition falls at the wrong moment, the change of movement is not made to time, and the physical expression of the rhythm is blurred.

Although feeling for rhythm is more or less latent in us all and can be developed, few have it naturally perfect. The method has many exercises which are of use in this connexion. By means of these the pupil is taught how to arrest movement suddenly or slowly, to move alternately forwards or backwards, to spring at a given signal, to lie down or stand up in the exact time of a bar of music—in each case with a minimum of muscular effort and without for a moment losing the feeling for each time-unit of the music.

MENTAL HEARING.
CONCENTRATION

Physical movements repeatedly performed create corresponding images in the brain; the stronger the feeling for the movement, i.e., the more the pupil concentrates while making that movement, the clearer will be the corresponding mental image, and the more fully will the sense for metre and rhythm be developed.

We might say that these movement images store up the innervations which bring about the actual movement. They are for the body and its movements what formulæ are for the mathematician.

Developed out of many movements they become a complete symbol for the rhythm expressed by the series of movements in question. Thus the pupil who knows how to march in time to a given rhythm has only to close his eyes and recall a clear image of the corresponding movements to experience the rhythm as clearly as if he were expressing it by marching. He simply continues to perform the movements mentally. If, however, his movements when actually realizing the rhythm are weak or confused, the corresponding mental images will be vague or incorrect, whilst movements which are dynamically clear guarantee the accuracy of the corresponding mental images and nerve-impulses.

In practice the exercise consists in first mastering a rhythm played, marching and beating time in the usual manner, then at *hopp* discontinuing all movement, either for a number of bars previously agreed upon or until the signal to resume is given by a second *hopp*. In this exercise the teacher ceases to play at the first *hopp*.

ANALYSIS AND DIVISION
OF TIME VALUES

The exercises of this group are designed to teach how to subdivide units of time into parts of varying number. At *hopp* the crotchet must be divided into quavers, triplets, semiquavers, etc., as may have been previously arranged, or instead of *hopp* the teacher may call *three, four*, etc., to indicate the subdivision which is to be expressed by the corresponding number of steps. Apart from their direct object, the exercises of this group are of value for the training which they give in poise; they might be classed equally well with the group under *Development of Mental Response*.

Here, too, belong exercises in the realization of syncopation in which, as the note is represented by the usual step, it comes off the beat, the latter being indicated by a knee-bend which, in quick time, becomes a mere suggestion of movement or is omitted, e.g.:

These exercises in syncopation are perhaps some of the most difficult in the method, as they demand an extraordinary control of inhibition. Individuals of musical ability often find them difficult at first, and their easy performance may be taken as evidence of a developed feeling for rhythm. As a rule children find these exercises easier than do adults.

REALIZATION OF TIME AND RHYTHM

The object here is to express by rhythmic movements and without hesitation rhythms perceived by the ear. The exactness of such expression will be in proportion to the number of movements of which the pupil has acquired automatic control. There is not time to analyse the music heard; the body must *realize* before the mind has a clear impression of the movement image, just as in reading, words are understood and pronounced without a clear

Beating 5/4 in canon without expression.

Beating 5/4 in canon with expression.

mental image of them being formed.

When the realization of a rhythm heard has become relatively easy, the pupil is taught to concentrate, by listening to, and forming a mental image of, a fresh rhythm while still performing the old one. In this manner he obtains facility in rendering automatic, groups of movements rhythmically arranged, and in keeping the mind free to take a fresh impression which in its turn can be rendered automatic.

Here again the process is analagous to that of reading, in which, while we are grasping the meaning of a sentence, the eye is already dealing with the next, preparing it in turn for comprehension.

DEVELOPMENT OF INDEPENDENT CONTROL OF THE LIMBS

Characteristic exercises of this group are: beating the same time with both arms but in canon, beating two different tempi with the arms while the feet march to one or other or perhaps march to yet a third time, e.g., the arms 3/4 and 4/4, the feet 5/4. There are, also, exercises in the analysis of a given time unit into various fractions simultaneously, c.g., in a 6/8 bar one arm may beat three to the bar, the other arm two, while the feet march six.

DOUBLE OR TRIPLE DEVELOPMENT OF RHYTHMS

These exercises are a physical preparation for what is known in music as the development of a theme. While the composers of fugues always use a double or quadruple development, the method introduces an entirely fresh element—the triple development, exercises in which are difficult but extremely valuable.

PLASTIC COUNTERPOINT AND COMPOUND RHYTHMS

In plastic counterpoint the arms realize the theme, i.e., make as many movements as there are notes, whilst the feet mark the counterpoint in crotchets, quavers, triplets or semiquavers.

A compound rhythm may be realized by the arms taking one rhythm, the feet another; or the rhythms of a three part canon may be expressed by simultaneous singing, beating with the arms and marching.

These exercises correspond in the sphere of physical expression to the technical exercises of instrumental work, for they teach the pupil to express simultaneously impressions of the most varying nature.

GRADATION OF MUSCULAR EFFORT.
PATHETIC ACCENT.
PLASTIC EXPRESSION

The exercises already dealt with have all the general purpose of developing feeling for rhythm by giving training in the physical expression of rhythms. Those in this last group aim at facility in making crescendos and decrescendos of innervation, in passing from one shade of expression to another, in co-ordinating movements, not only to the rhythm of the music played, but also to its feeling; they allow free play to individuality, to temperament, and give opportunity for that free self-expression for which the preceding exercises have provided facility.

Percy B. Ingham.

LESSONS AT HELLERAU

Monsieur Jaques-Dalcroze's lessons are full of vitality and entertainment, combined with the serious work in hand. No slacking is possible. He will perhaps open a rhythmic gymnastic lesson by playing a vigorous theme of one or two bars in a rhythm such as the following:

—which, as soon as it is grasped by the pupils, they begin to *realize,* that is, to mark the tempo with the arms, and to move the feet according to the notes. A note which contains more than one beat—for instance, the minim in the first bar—is shown by taking one step forward for the first beat and by a slight bend of the knee for the second beat. The next two crochets are represented by one step for each. A step is also taken for each quaver, but twice as quickly; for the dotted crochet, a step and a slight spring before the last quaver—all this while the arms are beating a steady four. After a short practice of these two bars, the master will glide into yet another rhythm, the pupils still realizing the first one, but at the same time listening and mentally registering the one being played, so as to be ready on the instant at the word of command, which is *hopp*, to change to the new rhythm. We will suppose it to be as follows:

This, it will be noticed, is in 3/4 time. The pupils become accustomed to dropping frequently into various times with the greatest ease. The three bars would then be realized consecutively, and this process will continue until perhaps there are six bars in all. These must all be so clear in the minds of the pupils, that at the word of command, one bar, or two bars, can be omitted on the instant, or be realized twice as quickly, or twice as slowly; or what is still more complicated, the arms can beat the time twice as slowly and the feet mark the notes twice as quickly. It seems incredibly difficult to do at first, but the same training of *thinking to time* occurs in every lesson, in improvisation and solfège, as well as in the rhythmic gymnastic lessons, and so the invaluable habits of concentrated thinking, of quick and definite action, and of control of mind over

6   See note, page 31

body, become established.

Each lesson is varied to a remarkable degree; in fact, Monsieur Jaques-Dalcroze seldom repeats himself. Every day he has new ideas, consisting of new movements, or of new uses for old ones, so that there is never a dull moment. It must be understood, however, that the alphabet and grammar of the movements remain the same, it is the combinations of them that are limitless. The music is, of course, always improvised.

THE AIR BATH.

THE COLLEGE: ENTRANCE HALL.

A word should be said on the subject of feeling two different rhythms at the same time. Every teacher knows the difficulty children have in playing three notes against four on the piano. The Hellerau children can with ease beat four with one arm and three with the other, or beat three with the arms and two or four with the feet, or *vice versa*. And this is not learnt in any mechanical way; the power for *feeling* two rhythms simultaneously is developed. Advanced pupils can realize three rhythms at the same time. They will perhaps mark one with the arms, another with the feet, and sing yet a third.

Another part of the work is to teach the pupils to express the type of music that is being played; this is technically known as "Plastic expression." The alphabet of this consists of twenty gestures with the arms, which can be done in many various combinations and in various positions, and by means of these any kind of emotion can be expressed. Perhaps the music will begin by being solemn and grand, becoming even tragic, and gradually the tones and melody will rise to cheerfulness, the rhythm will become more animated and the tone swell out again until a perfect ecstasy of joy is reached—and all the while the figures of the pupils are harmonising absolutely with the music, trained as they are to listen accurately to every note, every accent, every change of key and, above all, every rhythm. To the watcher such an exercise is effective and striking in the highest degree.

Realizing syncopated passages is a fine exercise for developing independence of movement in the arms and feet, as the feet move in between the beats of the arms. Let any one try to realize a simple measure in syncopation. For instance, take a bar of 4/4 time:

The first beat of the arms and the first step will come together, the second beat of the arms will come half-way between the second and third steps, the third beat half-way between the third and fourth steps, and the fourth beat half-way between the fourth and fifth steps, and this should be done with no contraction of muscle or appearance of effort.

Other exercises consist of beating various times in canon, that is, one arm beginning one beat later than the other; of beating different times with each arm, perhaps seven with one arm and three with the other; of marching to one rhythm and beating time to another; of simple marching and at the word of command taking one step backward, and then forward again; of marching the counterpoint of a rhythm. For instance, if the rhythm played be:

the counterpoint in crochets would be:

or if it is to be in quavers it would be:

The counterpoint can be filled in with triplets, semiquavers, or with notes of any other value.

Another good exercise is to take a simple rhythm and at the word of command realize it twice or three times as quickly or as slowly, the arms still beating in the first tempo. A simple example will make this clear:

twice as quickly would become:

The pupils are often asked to listen to what is played and then to realize it. It may be a series of four bars, each one in a different tempo, and all times are employed, including 5/4, 7/4, 9/3 and others which are somewhat exceptional. And so on *ad infinitum*.

From these suggestions something of the endless variety of exercises that may be devised can probably now be imagined.

As soon as movements become automatic they are used as units for building up more elaborate movements, and no time is wasted in doing merely mechanical exercises. In every detail of the method the brain is called into constant activity, and, lest any one should think that it would be easy for one pupil to copy another in doing the exercises, it should be stated that, if such a thing were attempted, it would end in the pupil becoming hopelessly confused, for if the mind once loses hold of the work in process it is very difficult to pick it up again.

The solfège lessons are chiefly for ear-training and practical harmony. In the elementary classes it is shown how scales and chords are formed, and where the tones and semitones occur. The pupils soon become able to tell, when three consecutive notes from any scale are played, what degrees of the scale they are, or may be. Scales are sung always beginning on C for every key and always to a rhythm. Here, again, the pupils have to think to time, for in the second scale, which would be that of F, if the flat scales

CLASS ROOMS.

were being sung, they have to remember that they are starting on the fifth note of the scale, and that the interval between the third and fourth notes of the scale is a semitone; that the third and fourth degrees in the key of F are A and B, and therefore the B has to be flattened in this scale, the other notes remaining the same. The whole cycle of scales is sung in this manner, each one commencing on C, or on C flat when necessary. The pupils are also practised in listening to a scale played and then saying in which key it is, judging it by the fall of the semitones.

Chords are sung analytically and in chorus, with their resolutions when needed, and this is followed by practice in hearing and naming chords.

Sight singing and transposition are by no means neglected, and there is practice in singing intervals, in singing a piece once or twice through and then from memory, or in another key, which is not so easy to do when the fixed *Do* is used. And always, whatever is being done, the pupils have to be prepared for the word *hopp*, to make any change which has been previously agreed on, e.g., to sing on the instant in a key a semitone lower, or to sing in thought only until the next *hopp*, when they sing aloud again. In these exercises, as in those of the rhythmic gymnastics, there is no end of the variety of combination possible. There is also opportunity for practice in conducting, and very interesting it is, in a children's class, to note with what assurance a small girl of perhaps

THE COLLEGE: INTERIORS.

seven or eight will beat time for the others to sing one of their songs, and also to note the various renderings each conductor will obtain of the same piece.

The improvisation on the piano is perhaps the most difficult part of the system to master. It may not be realized by all people that *every one can be taught to play original music*. There are cases in which the pupil is not naturally musical, and has had no previous knowledge of piano playing, but has learnt to improvise sufficiently well to give a good lesson in rhythmic gymnastics, which means no small degree of ability. This training is begun by making use of the simplest, i.e., the common, chords, and when these are known in every key, including those on the dominant, the pupil is expected to improvise a short piece of eight bars, the chief feature to be attended to being the rhythm, which has to be definite and played without hesitation. When perfect familiarity is obtained with the common chord of each key and with that of its dominant, another chord is learnt, that on the sub-dominant. With these three chords alone quite charming little pieces can be played, and gradually in this manner the pupil has at his command passing notes, appoggiaturas, cadences, and an unlimited number of chords and sequences. Then come the rules for modulating from one key to another, and equal facility in all keys is insisted on. Monsieur Jaques-Dalcroze's pupils learn to improvise with definite thought and meaning, nothing unrhythmical is ever allowed, nor any aimless meandering over the keyboard. For these lessons the pupils are divided into small groups of not more than six in each, and twice a week these groups are taken altogether by Monsieur Jaques-Dalcroze.

All branches of the work demand perfect concentration of thought and attention, and such invaluable mental training cannot be too highly prized, for it is fundamental to success in work of any kind, whatever it may be.

Ethel Ingham.

THE HOSTEL: INTERIORS.

LIFE AT HELLERAU

Surely never before has the world held better opportunities for studying and loving the beautiful and true. One need be but a few days in Hellerau in order to see some of the many advantages which a stay there has to offer. For young men and women searching for a profession in life; for those fresh from school while waiting to discover their natural bent; for adults who seek a change from their ordinary surroundings and who wish to improve in culture and in health; for musicians and students in art, for teachers of dancing, and for children of all ages, a course of study at the College in Hellerau contains advantages and opportunities which seem to exist in no other educational institution.

For the convenience of young girls there is a hall of residence, which will accommodate about forty-six students, the head of which is a cultured English lady of wide experience. There are also many small houses on adjoining land, in which the male students and those who are older can live. These may, and as a rule do, come to the Hostel for meals.

The home life in the Hostel is a cheerful one. The bedrooms are bright, containing just the necessary furniture, which of course includes a piano. There is a large and charmingly furnished room opening from the hall, known as the Diele, which serves as a general sitting-room for the students. The dining-room is equally delightful, and can be quickly converted into a ball-room for impromptu dances, or adapted for other entertainments. There is also a library; and throughout the whole house the

THE HOSTEL.

same good taste is displayed. Leading from the dining-room is a large terrace, with steps down into an attractive garden.

The day commences with the sounding of a gong at seven o'clock; the house is immediately alive, and some are off to the College for a Swedish gymnastic lesson before breakfast, others breakfast at half-past seven and have their lesson later. There is always a half hour of ordinary gymnastics to begin with. Then there will be a lesson in Solfège, one in Rhythmic Gymnastics, and one in Improvisation, each lasting for fifty minutes, with an interval of ten minutes between each lesson.

Dinner, which is at a quarter-past one, is followed by an hour for rest; and at three the energetic people begin practising. The afternoons are usually free, except twice a week, when there are lessons in "Plastic" and dancing from four till six, before which tea is served, or there may be extra lessons in rhythmic gymnastics for small groups of pupils who need further help, and students may obtain the use of a room for private practice together. In the afternoons, too, there is time and opportunity for any other extra study or lessons which are not included in the ordinary course, such as violin, solo singing, drawing or painting. Most of the students soon acquire wide interests, if they do not have them when they first come. Free afternoons may be spent in visiting the galleries and shops of Dresden. Whenever there is anything especially good in the way of a concert, or an opera or a classical play, there is always a party of enthusiasts going into town for it. The opera in Dresden, as in other parts of Germany, fortunately begins and ends early. Late hours are not encouraged at the Hostel—indeed, everybody is glad to retire early, for the work is absorbing and demands plenty of energy, especially if the full teachers' course be taken, with the hope of a diploma at the end of two years.

Supper is served at a quarter-past seven, and on two evenings a week those who wish to join the orchestral or choral societies have the pleasure of meeting together and practising under the direction of Monsieur Jaques-Dalcroze.

An atmosphere of enthusiasm and good-will permeates the social life. No community of the kind could have a more delightful spirit of unity than that which pervades the Jaques-Dalcroze School. All students are keen and anxious to live as full a life as possible, every one will willingly and unselfishly take time and trouble to help others who know less than themselves. The College has a unity born of kindred interests, and every one glows with admiration and esteem for the genius at the head, and for his wonderful method, whilst he himself simply radiates good-will and enthusiasm, and works harder than any one else in the place. He makes a point of knowing each one of his pupils personally, and remarkably quick he is in summing up the various temperaments and characters of those with whom he comes into contact.

The moral and mental tone of the College is pure and beautiful, indeed it could not well be otherwise, for the work in itself is an inspiration. A change is often observable in pupils after they have been but a few weeks in residence, a change which tells of more alertness of mind, of more animated purpose, and even of higher ideals and aims in life.

There are opportunities for the practice of many languages, for it is a cosmopolitan centre. Nearly all European nationalities are represented, but as yet the number of English people is not large. This, however, will not long remain so, for the Jaques-Dalcroze method needs only to be known in order to be as widely appreciated in Great Britain and the United States as it is on the Continent.

The lessons are given in German, though occasionally French is used to make clear anything that is not quite understood in the former tongue. English people who do not know either of these languages need not look upon this as an obstacle, for one quickly arrives at understanding sufficiently well to gain the benefit from the lessons, and there is always some one in the classes who will interpret when necessary.

The College itself is a fine example of the value of simplicity and space in architecture. Both without and within, the block of buildings is impressive, this effect being gained by an extreme

DRESDEN FROM HELLERAU.

simplicity of decoration. The most modern methods of heating and ventilating are provided, and there are large sun and air baths.

Completed in the spring of this year, and with accommodation for five hundred students, the settlement stands on high ground about four miles from Dresden, in an open, bracing, healthy spot, with charming walks in all directions. The views are extensive; to the south lie the Erzgebirge, to the south-east Saxon Switzerland, and, in a dip of the nearer hills, Dresden.

—Ethel Ingham.

THE VALUE OF
EURHYTHMICS TO ART

One of the most marked tendencies of modern aesthetic theory is to break down the barriers that convention has erected between the various arts. The truth is coming to be realized that the essential factor of poetry, painting, sculpture, architecture and music is really of the same quality, and that one art does not differ from another in anything but the method of its expression and the conditions connected with that method.

This common basis to the arts is more easily admitted than defined, but one important element in it—perhaps the only element that can be given a name—is rhythm. Rhythm of bodily movement, the dance, is the earliest form of artistic expression known. It is accompanied in nearly every case with rude music, the object being to emphasize the beat and rhythmic movement with sound. The quickness with which children respond to simple repetition of beat, translating the rhythm of the music into movement, is merely recurrence of historical development.

Words with the music soon follow, and from these beginnings—probably war-songs or religious chants—come song-poems and ultimately poetry as we know it to-day. The still more modern development of prose-writing, in the stylistic sense, is merely a step further.

The development on the other side follows a somewhat similar line. The rhythm of the dancing figure is reproduced in rude sculpture and bas-relief, and then in painting.

So we have, as it were, a scale of the arts, with music at its centre and prose-writing and painting at its two extremes. From end to end of the scale runs the unifying desire for rhythm.[7] To

---

7 For valuable help in these ideas I am indebted to Mr. J. W. Harvey. I should like to quote verbatim one or two remarks of his on the subject, taken from a recent letter: "Human motion gives the convergence of time (inner sense) and space (outer sense), the spirit and the body. Time, which we are in our inner selves, is more dissociable from us than space, which only our bodies have; the one (time) can be interpreted emotionally and directly by a time-sense; the other (space) symbolically, by a space-sense, which is sight."

speak of the rhythm of painting may seem fanciful, but I think that is only lack of familiarity. The expression is used here with no intention of metaphor. Great pictures have a very marked and real rhythm, of colour, of line, of feeling. The best prose-writing has equally a distinct rhythm.

There was never an age in the history of art when rhythm played a more important part than it does to-day. The teaching of M. Dalcroze at Hellerau is a brilliant expression of the modern desire for rhythm in its most fundamental form—that of bodily movement. Its nature and origin have been described elsewhere; it is for me to try and suggest the possibilities of its influence on every other art, and on the whole of life.

Let it be clearly understood from the first that the rhythmic training at Hellerau has an importance far deeper and more extended than is contained in its immediate artistic beauty, its excellence as a purely musical training, or its value to physical development. This is not a denial of its importance in these three respects. The beauty of the classes is amazing; the actor, as well as the designer of stage-effects, will come to thank M. Dalcroze for the greatest contribution to their art that any age can show. He has recreated the human body as a decorative unit. He has shown how men, women and children can group themselves and can be grouped in designs as lovely as any painted design, with the added charm of movement. He has taught individuals their own power of gracious motion and attitude. Musically and physically the

A PLASTIC EXERCISE.

results are equally wonderful. But the training is more than a mere musical education; it is also emphatically more than gymnastics.

Perhaps in the stress laid on individuality may be seen most easily the possibilities of the system. Personal effort is looked for in every pupil. Just as the learner of music must have the "opportunity of expressing his own musical impressions with the technical means which are taught him,"[8] so the pupil at Hellerau must come to improvise from the rhythmic sense innate in him, rhythms of his own.[9]

To take a joy in the beauty of the body, to train his mind to move graciously and harmoniously both in itself and in relation to those around him, finally, to make his whole life rhythmic—such an ideal is not only possible but almost inevitable to the pupil at Hellerau. The keenness which possesses the whole College, the delight of every one in their work, their comradeship, their lack of self-consciousness, their clean sense of the beauty of natural form, promises a new and more harmonious race, almost a realization of Rousseau's ideal, and with it an era of truly rhythmic artistic production.

That the soil is ready for the new seed may be shown by a moment's consideration of what I consider to be a parallel development in painting. There is in Munich a group of artists who call themselves Der Blaue Reiter. They are led by a Russian, Wassily Kandinsky, and a German, Franz Marc, and it is of Kandinsky's

8   Cf. supra, p. 28.

9   A good example of the fertility and variety of the individual effort obtained at Hellerau was seen at the Aufführung given on December 11, 1911. Two pupils undertook to realize a Prelude of Chopin, their choice falling by chance on the same Prelude. But hardly a movement of the two interpretations was the same. The first girl lay on the ground the whole time, her head on her arm, expressing in gentle movements of head, hands and feet, her idea of the music. At one point near the end, with the rising passion of the music, she raised herself on to her knees; then sank down again to her full length.

The second performer stood upright until the very end. At the most intense moment her arms were stretched above her head; at the close of the music she was bowed to the ground, in an attitude expressive of the utmost grief. In such widely different ways did the same piece of music speak to the individualities of these two girls.

art that I propose to speak. Kandinsky is that rare combination, an artist who can express himself in both words and paint. His book—*Über das Geistige in der Kunst*[10]—is an interesting and subtle piece of aesthetic philosophy. His painting is a realization of the attempt to paint music. He has isolated the emotion caused by line and colour from the external association of idea. All form in the ordinary representative sense is eliminated. But form there is in the deeper sense, the shapes and rhythms of the *innerer Notwendigkeit*, and with it, haunting, harmonious colour. To revert to a former metaphor, painting has been brought into the centre of the scale. As Kandinsky says in his book: "Shades of colour, like shades of sound, are of a much subtler nature, cause much subtler vibrations of the spirit than can ever be given by words." It is to achieve this finer utterance, to establish a surer and more expressive connexion between spirit and spirit, that Kandinsky is striving. His pictures are visions, beautiful abstractions of colour and line which he has lived himself, deep down in his inmost soul. He is intensely individual, as are all true mystics; at the same time the spirit of his work is universal.

In this, then, as in so much else, Kandinsky and Dalcroze are advancing side by side. They are leading the way to the truest art, and ultimately to the truest life of all, which is a synthesis of the collective arts and emotions of all nations, which is, at the same time, based on individuality, because it represents the inner being of each one of its devotees.

—Michael T. H. Sadler.

---

10 *Über das Geistige in der Kunst*. Piper Verlag, München, 3 Marks. See also vol. i. of *der Blaue Reiter*. Piper Verlag, 10 Marks.